CODEPENCY

Table of Contents

Introduction   1

What Is Codependency?   5

Symptoms Of Codependency   11

Important Questionnaire To Identify Signs Of Co-Dependency   31

Patterns Of Codependency   35

Characteristics Of Codependency   41

Statements Of Truth To Help Support Recovery   49

Identifying Codependent Relationships   53

Causes Of Codependency   55

How To Stop Being Codependent   63

Codependency And Addiction   97

How Does A Codependent Relationship Develop?   101

Codependence Vs. Dependence   107

Styles Of Codependent Relationships   111

What Is A Dysfunctional Family And How Does It Lead To Co-Dependency?   115

Conclusion   125

INTRODUCTION

Codependency refers to a mental, emotional, physical, and/or spiritual reliance on a partner, friend, or family member."The term was originally coined in the 1950s in the context of Alcoholics Anonymous to support partners of individuals who abused substances, and who were entwined in the toxic lives of those they cared for," says Dr. Renee Exelbert, a licensed psychologist and author based in New York.

The term codependency has been around for almost four decades. Although it originally applied to spouses of alcoholics, first called co-alcoholics, research revealed that the characteristics of codependents were much more prevalent in the general population than had been imagined.

In fact, they found that if you were raised in a dysfunctional family or had an ill parent, it's likely that you're codependent. Don't feel bad if that includes you. Most families in America are dysfunctional, so that covers just about everyone; you're in the majority!

This is still true — but today, codependency covers a much broader spectrum.

Codependency is not a clinical diagnosis or a formally categorized personality disorder on its own. Generally speaking, codependency incorporates aspects of attachment style patterns developed in early childhood, and it can also overlap with other personality disorders, including dependent personality disorder.

The term 'codependency' is often used casually to describe relationships where a person is needy or dependent upon another person.

There is much more to this term than everyday clinginess. Codependent relationships are far more extreme than this. A person who is codependent will plan their entire life around pleasing the other person or the enabler.

Some mental health professionals argue that codependency should be considered an official mental illness. This does not mean that codependency isn't real or is inconsequential—far from it. Codependency can be debilitating.

A codependent person puts their own needs aside and becomes hyper-vigilant about meeting the needs of another person, to the point that their life revolves around this person, creating a one-sided relationship that is destructive and dysfunctional for both parties.

Codependency involves sacrificing one's personal needs to try to meet the needs of others. Someone who is codependent has an extreme focus outside themselves. Their thoughts and actions revolve around other people, such as spouses or relatives.

Codependency often appears in relationships that are unbalanced and unhealthy. A person with codependency often tries to save others from themselves. They may get hurt trying to "cure" a partner's addictions or abusive behaviors.

Codependency does not qualify as a mental health diagnosis, mostly because the symptoms are so widely applicable. Yet, it can still cause severe distress. Codependency may lead a person to develop other mental health concerns such as anxiety. A therapist can help a person reduce codependent behaviors and develop healthier relationships.

WHAT IS CODEPENDENCY?

Co-dependency is a learned behavior that can be passed down from one generation to another. It is an emotional and behavioral condition that affects an individual's ability to have a healthy, mutually satisfying relationship. It is also known as "relationship addiction" because people with codependency often form or maintain relationships that are one-sided, emotionally destructive, and/or abusive. The disorder was first identified about ten years ago as the result of years of studying interpersonal relationships in families of alcoholics. Co-dependent behavior is learned by watching and imitating other family members who display this type of behavior.

Codependency is an addiction that is not as obvious as gambling, alcoholism, and substance abuse. Similar to working, caretaking seems positive until it gets compulsive and out of hand.

Even though codependency is a problem that affects many people, one might struggle with codependency their whole life and never know about it. That's because denial is a natural self-protection strategy that codependents adopt. Codependents might not be aware of their own behavior and control patterns.

Codependency is a two-sided coin of "give" and "take."

One individual tends to fill the caregiver role: They'll step in and help a loved one who's experiencing difficulties. This impulse often stems from good intentions – after all, the desire to help others is human nature. But when such actions become the go-to response, the dynamic may become potentially enabling to its recipient.

On the other side is the individual receiving this attention. Such a symbiotic dynamic can cause the "care taken" individual to foster reliance – and they may start to fall into a habit of depending on the caregiver to "bail them out," so to speak.

Although codependency has long been associated with substance abuse and chronic illnesses – e.g., child-caring and taking responsibility for their alcoholic parent – it can apply to other types of relationships as well. Romantic partners, friends, and family members can all fall into codependent patterns.

Furthermore, codependency is not limited to relationships that involve living with someone who has an addiction. If you are in a relationship with a narcissist or someone with borderline personality, you might show signs of codependency too. Even in friendship and work relationships, one might be codependent too.

In its simplest terms, a codependent relationship is when one partner needs the other partner, who in turn needs to be needed. This circular relationship is the basis of what experts refer to when they describe the "cycle" of codependency.

The codependent's self-esteem and self-worth will come only from sacrificing themselves for their partner, who is only too glad to receive their sacrifices.

A codependent relationship is a kind of dysfunctional relationship where one person is a caretaker, and the other person takes advantage. Codependent relationships are extremely common among people with substance use issues. Typically, one partner will take care of the other to the extent of enabling that partner's addictive behavior.

Often, the caretaker is raised in a family with an addicted parent and learns to placate that parent in order to make life easier for her and her siblings. This is often the oldest child, and she may repeat the pattern in her own relationships as an adult. Codependency is not good for either partner. It allows one partner to sink deeper in addiction while forcing the other partner to completely forgo her own wants and needs in order to care for the other.

Fast facts on codependency:

Codependent relationships can be between friends, romantic partners, or family members.

Often, the relationship includes emotional or physical abuse.

Friends and family members of a codependent person may recognize that something is wrong.

Like any mental or emotional health issue, treatment requires time and effort, as well as the help of a clinician.

SYMPTOMS OF CODEPENDENCY

The following is a list of symptoms of codependency and being in a codependent relationship. You don't need to have them all to qualify as codependent.

- **Low self-esteem**

Feeling that you're not good enough or comparing yourself to others are signs of low self-esteem. The tricky thing about self-esteem is that some people think highly of themselves, but it's only a disguise — they actually feel unlovable or inadequate. Underneath, usually hidden from consciousness, are feelings of shame. Guilt and perfectionism often go along with low self-esteem. If everything is perfect, you don't feel bad about yourself.

Typically, neither person in a codependent relationship has very good self-esteem. One person needs the approval of the other or at least needs to be of service to the other to have a sense of purpose. The other person has low self-esteem as a result of having to depend on someone else to meet material needs and needing validation from that person. The dependent person is often controlling out of a basic sense of insecurity that the other person might leave.

A person who's codependent will likely feel like their personality depends on the other person. You may not feel like you know what you really like or who you really are. Instead, your focus is only on things the other person likes or dislikes.

- **People-pleasing**

It's fine to want to please someone you care about, but codependents usually don't think they have a choice. Saying "No" causes them anxiety. Some codependents have a hard time saying "No" to anyone. They go out of their way and sacrifice their own needs to accommodate other people.

When you are codependent, you may have a deep-seated fear that the other person is going to leave you. Most of what you do in the relationship will be intended to make sure the other person doesn't leave. This can include hiding your own feelings, lying, and supporting the other person in unhealthy behaviors.

It's normal to want people to like you, and we all want our loved ones to be happy, but there's a difference between these normal tendencies and having to please people all the time. People pleasers often feel like they have no choice but to keep other people happy. They don't like to say no even when pleasing others substantially interferes with their own wants and needs.

- **Poor boundaries**

Boundaries are sort of an imaginary line between you and others. It divides up what's yours and somebody else's, and that applies not only to your body, money, and belongings but also to your feelings, thoughts, and needs. That's especially where codependents get into trouble. They have blurry or weak boundaries. They feel responsible for other people's feelings and problems or blame their own on someone else. Some codependents have rigid boundaries. They are closed off and withdrawn, making it hard for other people to get close to them. Sometimes, people flip back and forth between having weak boundaries and having rigid ones.

- **Reactivity**

A consequence of poor boundaries is that you react to everyone's thoughts and feelings. If someone says something you disagree with, you either believe it or become defensive. You absorb their words because there's no boundary. With a boundary, you'd realize it was just their opinion and not a reflection of you and not feel threatened by disagreements.

When your identity is based on pleasing others, and you feel responsible for everyone's wellbeing, you might find yourself reacting to situations rather than acting out of your own volition. You might find yourself being defensive or easily internalizing criticism. This is a result partly of having lost touch with your own wants and needs, which makes it harder to be proactive. It is also partly a result of your inability to set boundaries so that you feel responsible for someone else's feelings.

- **Caretaking**

Another effect of poor boundaries is that if someone else has a problem, you want to help them to the point that you give up yourself. It's natural to feel empathy and sympathy for someone, but codependents start putting other people ahead of themselves. In fact, they need to help and might feel rejected if another person doesn't want help. Moreover, they keep trying to help and fix the other person, even when that person clearly isn't taking their advice.

A major sign of codependency is when you feel like you have to take care of everyone all the time. This typically comes from childhood; when the caretaker learns, there may be really bad consequences from failing to take care of a parent's needs. As a result, she may feel compelled to take care of others, especially a partner, not so much out of affection, but from the fear that something bad will happen if she doesn't. Most people can get by fairly well on their own, and feeling like things will go terribly wrong if you don't take care of them is often a sign of codependency.

- **Control**

Control helps codependents feel safe and secure. Everyone needs some control over events in their life. You wouldn't want to live in constant uncertainty and chaos, but for codependents, control limits their ability to take risks and share their feelings. Sometimes they have an addiction that either helps them loosen up, like alcoholism, or helps them hold their feelings down, like workaholism so that they don't feel out of control. Codependents also need to control those close to them because they need other people to behave in a certain way to feel okay. In fact, people-pleasing and care-taking can be used to control and manipulate people. Alternatively, codependents are bossy and tell you what you should or shouldn't do. This is a violation of someone else's boundary.

- **Dysfunctional communication**

Codependents have trouble when it comes to communicating their thoughts, feelings, and needs. Of course, if you don't know what you think, feel or need, this becomes a problem. Other times, you know, but you won't own up to your truth.

You're afraid to be truthful because you don't want to upset someone else. Instead of saying, "I don't like that," you might pretend that it's okay or tell someone what to do. Communication becomes dishonest and confusing when you try to manipulate the other person out of fear.

A codependent mindset makes it hard to communicate effectively. The caregiver is often unaware of her own wants and needs, and when she is aware of them, she may be reluctant to express them. She may feel like caring for the other person is the most important thing, or she may fear upsetting the other person by asserting herself.

The dependent person may be in the habit of communicating dishonestly, more interested in maintaining control than in actually communicating. Communication is another crucial skill to learn in family therapy. Both people have to learn to communicate honestly and effectively.

- **Obsessions**

Codependents have a tendency to spend their time thinking about other people or relationships. This is caused by their dependency and anxietiesand fears. They can also become obsessed when they think they've made or might make a "mistake."Sometimes you can lapse into fantasy about how you'd like things to be or about someone you love as a way to avoid the pain of the present. This is one way to stay in denial, discussed below, but it keeps you from living your life.

- **Dependency**

Codependents need other people to like them to feel okay about themselves. They're afraid of being rejected or abandoned, even if they can function on their own. Others need always to be in a relationship because they feel depressed or lonely when they're by themselves for too long. This trait makes it hard for them to end a relationship, even when the relationship is painful or abusive. One of the primary signs of potential codependency is feeling like you can't live without the other person. People with codependent tendencies often feel a compulsive need to keep themselves connected with the other person. You might feel like the other person is so important to you that you have to hide your real thoughts and opinions to make sure they like you.

Of course, dependency plays a major role in codependency. Each person needs the other for something. One person needs her material needs to be met because addiction or other issues have impeded her autonomy, and the other person needs validation and a sense of purpose from taking care of someone. In a way, it's a tradeoff, but it also limits both people involved.

Another potential risk factor for codependency is relying entirely on one person for your emotional needs. You may not have a large social circle or have others you feel comfortable spending time with.

Codependent people tend to focus so heavily on one person that they don't have time to spend with other people who are important to them.

After a while in a codependent relationship, you may start to resent the other person. More importantly, you'll resent them while feeling like you can't live without them or like they can't live without you. This is the biggest sign that your relationship is unhealthy and potentially codependent.

They end up feeling trapped.

- **Denial**

One of the problems people face in getting help for codependency is that they're in denial about it, meaning that they don't face their problem. Usually, they think the problem is someone else or the situation. They either keep complaining or trying to fix the other person, or go from one relationship or job to another and never own up to the fact that they have a problem. Codependents also deny their feelings and needs. Often, they don't know what they're feeling and are instead focused on what others are feeling. The same thing goes for their needs. They pay attention to other people's needs and not their own. They might be in denial of their need for space and autonomy. Although some codependents seem needy, others act like they're self-sufficient when it comes to needing help. They won't reach out and have trouble receiving. They are in denial of their vulnerability and need for love and intimacy.

- **Problems with intimacy**

Although sexual dysfunction often is a reflection of an intimacy problem. Because of the shame and weak boundaries, you might fear that you'll be judged, rejected, or left. On the other hand, you may fear being smothered in a relationship and losing your autonomy. You might deny your need for closeness and feel that your partner wants too much of your time; your partner complains that you're unavailable, but he or she denies his or her need for separateness.

- **Painful emotions**

Codependency creates stress and leads to painful emotions. Shame and low self-esteem create anxiety and fear about being judged, rejected, or abandoned; making mistakes; being a failure; feeling trapped by being close or being alone.

The other symptoms lead to feelings of anger and resentment, depression, hopelessness, and despair. When the feelings are too much, you can feel numb.

- **You take too much responsibility for your partner.**

Of course, in any relationship, you want to care for your partner. But taking on too much responsibility for their well-being is another sign of codependency. "In order to feel in control and 'okay,' you look to manage and take care of your partner's behavior,." If your partner is drinking, you'll always be the one reminding them not to drink or cleaning up any problems they may get themselves into.

- **You gravitate toward people who need you.**

You may tend to date people who need help. It's all in an effort to take responsibility for people and rescue them. This is why codependent people are often attracted to those who have addictions, like drinking or gambling. You may also put yourself in peril to help them via taking on a gambling debt, dipping into your savings to support them, or getting into a car with them when you know they're a reckless driver.

- **You never get your way.**

Let's say you feel like staying in, but your partner wants to go out and hit the bars. In a healthy relationship, you might reach a compromise—you'll stay in tonight but make plans to go out tomorrow. In a codependent relationship, your partner might cut you down ("God, you're so boring, this is why you have no friends"), causing you to cave ("Fine, we'll go out, it doesn't matter anyway"). While it seems like a minor problem, it may be one of the many examples of how your needs aren't acknowledged or valued.

- **They've told you you're a "nag."**

If you feel like you always have to keep close tabs on your partner and tell them what not to do, you may be codependent. Try taking a step back and letting them make their own decisions. How does that feel? Impossible because you know they'll mess up?

- **You'd describe your partner as "immature."**

If your partner is resisting being a responsible adult and you're taking care of them—paying the bills while they avoid getting a job, for instance—your relationship may be codependent. The key tip-off: If you bring up the problem (why aren't you sending out more resumes?), you get barked at. You may also find yourself making excuses for his or her behavior to your friends.

- **You only fight about one thing.**

While this sounds like it'd be a good thing—you're in relative harmony except for when "xyz" comes up—it's another sign of codependency. You may find yourself saying things like "he/she/our relationship is perfect except for when they…" If you're always angry at certain behaviors and your arguments center around one fight or issue in particular (and tend to blow up), it may be time to reevaluate your relationship and what it's doing for you.

- **You do things for them they should do on their own.**

"This is one of the easiest ways to fall into a codependent relationship,." It goes back to the idea of needing to feel needed, which often stems from relationships in your childhood. While it can be sweet to treat your partner with breakfast in bed one morning, it's important not to make a habit out of doing simple things, like waking the person up or cleaning up their messes, on a continual basis. "Treating your partner like a child creates a toxic codependent relationship,."

- **You talk about your partner's issues more than your own.**

When your world begins to revolve around your partner's unhappiness at work, family drama, or financial troubles, it's unhealthy for you. "Your life is almost like a reflection of theirs, so their problems, worries, and anxieties are your primary importance,." If you and your partner's conversations always center on what's going on with them and never on anything you're dealing with, you could be in a codependent relationship.

Likewise, if you find yourself only telling your friends about your partner (and not just when the two of you are going through a rough patch—that's totally normal, and even healthy, to discuss with friends) and not updating them on your own life, it's likely that there's some codependency going on. "It might be a sign that you feel like you don't exist away from your partner,"

- **You struggle to identify your own emotions.**

If you find yourself checking in with your partner to gauge exactly how you feel about a situation, it can signal a codependent relationship. It's great to be on the same page as your partner emotionally, but this can go too far. "Because your feelings and thoughts are so unified with little to no boundaries, it can be challenging to identify where yours end and theirs begins,." It's a problem if you're giving so much of yourself that you forget to check in on your own feelings. This can often continue for a long time before you realize that you aren't in touch with your own emotions.

- **You check in with your partner before doing anything.**

Communication is key when making important life decisions, but some choices (like your career, for example) are meant for you alone. Of course, certain things will have an effect on the relationship, but other things won't, so you're free to fly solo. "You're giving someone a lot of power by continually checking with your partner before you do anything,." "Someone who is checking in at all times, asking if things are okay, is someone who doubts their power in the relationship,." Your relationship is likely codependent if you can't seem to shake that habit.

One question you should ask yourself is: how much time in a given day do you spend thinking about your relationship? If the answer is most of the time, your relationship is probably codependent.

Also, if you are constantly seeking reassurance, asking questions like, "Do you love me? " and "Do you promise you won't leave me?," you may be codependent.

Other symptoms of codependency include putting your partner on a pedestal, idealizing that person despite his or her faults, and making excuses for your loved one when he or she neglects important tasks. Givers often think they're helping their partners when in reality, they're actually preventing them from personal growth.

Important Questionnaire To Identify Signs Of Co-dependency

This condition appears to run in different degrees, whereby the intensity of symptoms is on a spectrum of severity, as opposed to an all or nothing scale. Please note that only a qualified professional can make a diagnosis of co-dependency; not everyone experiencing these symptoms suffers from co-dependency.

1. Do you keep quiet to avoid arguments?

2. Are you always worried about others' opinions of you?

3. Have you ever lived with someone with an alcohol or drug problem?

4. Have you ever lived with someone who hits or belittles you?

5. Are the opinions of others more important than your own?

6. Do you have difficulty adjusting to changes at work or home?

7. Do you feel rejected when significant others spend time with friends?

8. Do you doubt your ability to be who you want to be?

9. Are you uncomfortable expressing your true feelings to others?

10. Have you ever felt inadequate?

11. Do you feel like a "bad person" when you make a mistake?

12. Do you have difficulty taking compliments or gifts?

13. Do you feel humiliated when your child or spouse makes a mistake?

14. Do you think people in your life would go downhill without your constant efforts?

15. Do you frequently wish someone could help you get things done?

16. Do you have difficulty talking to people in authority, such as the police or your boss?

17. Are you confused about who you are or where you are going with your life?

18. Do you have trouble saying "no" when asked for help?

19. Do you have trouble asking for help?

20. Do you have so many things going at once that you can't do justice to any of them?

If you identify with several of these symptoms; are dissatisfied with yourself or your relationships; you should consider seeking professional help. Arrange for a diagnostic evaluation with a licensed physician or psychologist experienced in treating co-dependency.

PATTERNS OF CODEPENDENCY

> ➢ **Denial Patterns**

Codependents often...

- ✓ Have difficulty identifying what they are feeling
- ✓ Minimize, alter, or deny how they truly feel.
- ✓ Perceive themselves as completely unselfish and dedicated to the well- being of others
- ✓ Lack empathy for the feelings and needs of others.
- ✓ Label others with their negative traits.
- ✓ They think they can take care of themselves without any help from others.
- ✓ Mask pain in various ways, such as anger, humor, or isolation.
- ✓ Express negativity or aggression in indirect and passive ways.
- ✓ Do not recognize the unavailability of those people to whom they are attracted.

> ➢ **Low Self-esteem Patterns**

Codependents often...

- ✓ Have difficulty making decisions.
- ✓ Judge what they think, say, or do harshly, as never good enough.

- ✓ Are embarrassed to receive recognition, praise, or gifts.
- ✓ Value others' approval of their thinking, feelings, and behavior over their own.
- ✓ Do not perceive themselves as lovable or worthwhile persons.
- ✓ Seek recognition and praise to overcome feeling less than.
- ✓ Have difficulty admitting a mistake.
- ✓ They need to appear to be right in the eyes of others and may even lie to look good.
- ✓ They are unable to identify or ask for what they need and want.
- ✓ Perceive themselves as superior to others.
- ✓ Look to others to provide their sense of safety.
- ✓ Have difficulty getting started, meeting deadlines, and completing projects.
- ✓ Have trouble setting healthy priorities and boundaries.

➤ **Compliance Patterns**

Codependents often...

- ✓ They are extremely loyal, remaining in harmful situations too long.
- ✓ Compromise their own values and integrity to avoid rejection or anger.

- ✓ Put aside their own interests in order to do what others want.
- ✓ Are hypervigilant regarding the feelings of others and take on those feelings.
- ✓ They are afraid to express their beliefs, opinions, and feelings when they differ from those of others.
- ✓ Accept sexual attention when they want to love.
- ✓ Make decisions without regard to the consequences.
- ✓ Give up their truth to gain the approval of others or to avoid change.

> **Control Patterns**

Codependents often...

- ✓ Believe people are incapable of taking care of themselves.
- ✓ Attempt to convince others what to think, do, or feel.
- ✓ Freely offer advice and direction without being asked.
- ✓ Become resentful when others decline their help or reject their advice.
- ✓ Lavish gifts and favors on those they want to influence.
- ✓ Use sexual attention to gain approval and acceptance.
- ✓ Have to feel needed in order to have a relationship with others.
- ✓ Demand that their needs be met by others.

- ✓ Use charm and charisma to convince others of their capacity to be caring and compassionate.
- ✓ Use blame and shame to exploit others emotionally.
- ✓ Refuse to cooperate, compromise, or negotiate.
- ✓ Adopt an attitude of indifference, helplessness, authority, or rage to manipulate outcomes.
- ✓ Use recovery jargon in an attempt to control the behavior of others.
- ✓ Pretend to agree with others to get what they want.

➤ **Avoidance Patterns**

Codependents often...

- ✓ Act in ways that invite others to reject, shame, or express anger toward them.
- ✓ Judge harshly what others think, say, or do.
- ✓ Avoid emotional, physical, or sexual intimacy as a way to maintain distance.
- ✓ Allow addictions to people, places, and things to distract them from achieving intimacy in relationships.
- ✓ Use indirect or evasive communication to avoid conflict or confrontation.
- ✓ Diminish their capacity to have healthy relationships by declining to use the tools of recovery.
- ✓ Suppress their feelings or needs to avoid feeling vulnerable.

- ✓ Pull people toward them, but when others get close, push them away.
- ✓ Refuse to give up their self-will to avoid surrendering to a power greater than themselves.
- ✓ Believe displays of emotion are a sign of weakness.
- ✓ Withhold expressions of appreciation.

CHARACTERISTICS OF CODEPENDENCY

You are hyper-aware of other peoples' needs, so you become a caretaker to avoid being blamed for other people's unhappiness and/or to feed your self-esteem by making them happy.

You believe that love and pain are synonymous. This becomes a familiar feeling, so you continue to allow friends, family, and romantic relationships to behave poorly and treat you with disrespect.

Your self-esteem and self-worth are dependent on those you are trying to please. Your self-worth is based on whether or not other people are happy with what you can do for them. You over-schedule yourself with other people's priorities to prove you are worthy.

You people-please. As a child, having a preference or speaking up resulted in being punished. You quickly learned that letting others have their way spared you from that pain. You're afraid to upset or disappoint others, which often leads to over-extending yourself to avoid negative feedback.

You always put others' needs before your own. You feel guilty if you don't follow through, even if it means sacrificing your well-being. You ignore your own feelings and needs, reasoning that others are more deserving of your time and help.

You lack boundaries. You have trouble speaking up for yourself and saying NO. You allow people to take advantage of your kindness because you don't want to be responsible for their hurt their feelings.

You feel guilty and ashamed about things you didn't even do. You were blamed for everything as a child, so you continue to expect everyone to believe this about you now.

You're always on edge. This is due to growing up in an environment lacking security and stability. While healthy parents protect their children from harm and danger, dysfunctional parents are the source of fear for their children and distort their self-perception.

You feel unworthy and lonely. You were always told you are not good enough and everything is your fault. The dysfunctional parent conditioned you to believe that you are of no value to anyone, leaving you with no one to turn to.

You don't trust anyone. If you can't even trust your own parents, who can you trust? Your unhealthy childhood conditioning leads you to believe that you do not deserve honesty or to feel safe.

You won't let others help you. You'd rather give than receive. You try to avoid having to owe someone for the help they give you or have the favor used against you. You'd also rather do it yourself because others can't do it your way.

You are controlling. You were conditioned to believe that you are a "good boy/girl" if those around you are OK. So when life feels overwhelming, you try to find order by controlling others instead of fixing what needs repairs in your own life.

You have unrealistic expectations for yourself as a result of the harsh criticism you constantly received as a child.

You complain about how unhappy your life has become, then quickly take it back to protect your ego, trapping you in an unending cycle of the complaint/deny.

You melt into others. You have difficulty separating yourself from other people's feelings, needs, and even identities. You define your identity in relation to others while lacking a solid sense of self.

You are a martyr. You are always giving without receiving, then feel angry, resentful, and taken advantage of.

You are passive-aggressive. You feel angry and resentful and complain about having to do everything – while you continue doing everything on your own.

You fear criticism, rejection, and failure, so you procrastinate on your own dreams and goals. Instead, you manage and control people's plans and extract fulfillment when they succeed.

These self-destructive thoughts, emotions, and behaviors are based on distorted beliefs that developed as a result of emotional abuse during your childhood. As a helpless child, it was necessary to adapt these behaviors in order to survive.

Studies show codependency is common in adults who were raised by parents with substance abuse problems, who live in chronic stressful family environments, who have children with behavior problems, and who care for the chronically ill. Women are more likely to be codependent than men.

Co-dependents have low self-esteem and look for anything outside of themselves to make them feel better. They find it hard to "be themselves." Some try to feel better through alcohol, drugs, or nicotine - and become addicted. Others may develop compulsive behaviors like workaholism, gambling, or indiscriminate sexual activity.

They have good intentions. They try to take care of a person who is experiencing difficulty, but the caretaking becomes compulsive and defeating. Co-dependents often take on a martyr's role and become "benefactors" to an individual in need. A wife may cover for her alcoholic husband, a mother may make excuses for a truant child, or a father may "pull some strings" to keep his child from suffering the consequences of delinquent behavior.

The problem is that these repeated rescue attempts allow the needy individual to continue on a destructive course and to become even more dependent on the unhealthy caretaking of the "benefactor." As this reliance increases, the co-dependent develops a sense of reward and satisfaction from "being needed." When the caretaking becomes compulsive, the co-dependent feels choiceless and helpless in the relationship but is unable to break away from the cycle of behavior that causes it. Co-dependents view themselves as victims and are attracted to that same weakness in love and friendship relationships.

Individuals in the helping professions are also more likely to be in codependent relationships. It's estimated that one-third of nurses have moderate to severe levels of codependency. Nurses need to be sensitive to the needs of others and often need to set aside their own feelings for the good of their patients.

They may also find validation in their ability to care for others, and that need may spill over into their personal lives.

Statements of Truth to Help Support Recovery

1. I have the right to my own thoughts, feelings, and values. You don't have to be like everyone else. And you don't have to always agree with everyone else. You are your own person and entitled (just like everyone else) to your own sense of self. Don't let differences in opinions make you feel like you're wrong. Your true friends and family will still love you whether or not they agree with anything you do or say!

2. The only person I have control over is myself. When you take control of other people, you're taking away their right to their own thoughts, feelings, and behaviors – that's not fair. Shift your focus back on yourself and get to know yourself better. It's time to discover what YOU want and need in life!

3. I don't have to own other people's issues. Just as it's no one else's responsibility to fix your problems, it's not your responsibility to solve anyone else's. Let yourself off the hook and work on being your best self instead!

4. Saying NO does not make me selfish or unkind. There is nothing wrong or mean about declining, refusing, or disagreeing. No is a way you communicate your preference – just like answering, "Yes." That's it. It's understandable if the person you are answering to is disappointed, but it's their responsibility to get over it—those who flatly refuse to accept your decision need to step back and work on their own boundaries.

5. I deserve to be just as kind to myself as I am to others. You are worthy of as much love, kindness, and compassion as the most celebrated people on our planet. Do not allow anyone to convince you that you deserve less. Those suggestions usually come from people with hurtful intentions.

6. I don't have to sacrifice my well-being to care for others. You have the right and responsibility to care for and protect yourself in order to continue performing at your highest capacity. This not only benefits you but those who depend on you. Because when you're at your best, you can better care for those around you.

7. My self-worth isn't based on external approval. Self-worth is the value you place on yourself. It's completely independent of what anyone else thinks about you or what you can do for anyone else. So take a deep breath and appreciate the heck out of who you are!

8. Having my own preferences and choosing what feels right for me is not selfish. Codependents tend to believe doing what's right for them is selfish. This is why setting and enforcing boundaries is necessary. Healthy boundaries give you a safe place to comfortably step into your authentic self!

9. I can be loved simply for who I am. You don't have to fit into everyone's mold in order to be loved. That's not real love – it's being loved for who you appear to be. There's nothing wrong with being an acquired taste. Relax and be yourself. This will draw in people who genuinely appreciate and love you.

Identifying Codependent Relationships

While codependency isn't something that shows up in a lab test or a brain scan, there are some questions that you can ask yourself to help spot codependent behavior.

1. Do you feel compelled to help other people?
2. Do you try to control events and how other people should behave?
3. Are you afraid to let other people be who they are and allow events to happen naturally?
4. Do you feel ashamed of who you are?
5. Do you try to control events and people through helplessness, guilt, coercion, threats, advice-giving, manipulation, or domination?
6. Do you have a hard time asking others for help?
7. Do you feel compelled or forced to help people solve their problems (i.e., offering advice)?
8. Do you often hide what you are really feeling?
9. Do you avoid openly talking about problems?
10. Do you push painful thoughts and feelings out of your awareness?
11. Do you blame yourself and put yourself down?

If you answer yes to any of these questions, it may be a sign of codependent behavior patterns in your relationships.

Identifying these patterns is an important step in learning how to stop being codependent.

"Individuals can also assume they are in a codependent relationship if people around them have given them feedback that they are too dependent on their partner or if they have a desire, at times, for more independence but feel an even stronger conflict when they attempt to separate in any way," says psychologist Seth Meyers.

"They'll feel anxiety more consistently than any other emotion in the relationship," Meyers says, "and they'll spend a great deal of time and energy either trying to change their partner or... trying to conform to their partner's wishes."

CAUSES OF CODEPENDENCY

Codependency can often be traced back to childhood, to the relationships we had with our parents (or primary caretakers). It usually happens when we had parents who were either overly protective or under protective.

Overprotective parents hold their children back from building the confidence needed to move out into the world. There might have been anxieties around trying new things ("you can't go on the slide because you'll hurt yourself") or you might have been so mollycoddled that you never learned how to do basic tasks like cooking or washing your clothes.

hese kinds of parent-child relationships are often enmeshed as well, with limited personal boundaries. Perhaps a parent treated you more like a friend, sharing secrets with you, over-involving themselves in your life, and including you in daily decision-making. The parent keeps the child dependent on them by reinforcing dependent behaviors and discouraging independent behaviors. In these cases, aside from not developing the confidence to take care of yourself, there might also be a pang of guilt attached to even wanting or needing your own life.

Once people recognize that they have codependent traits, they often begin to wonder where these codependent tendencies came from. Why are some people susceptible to codependency in their adult relationships? What causes codependency? Why is it so hard to break free from codependent relationships?

While the answers aren't the same for everyone, for most people, it begins in childhood. This is important because children are extremely impressionable. Young children don't have the cognitive abilities or life experiences to realize that the relationships they are seeing and experiencing aren't healthy, that their parents aren't always right, that parents lie and manipulate and lack the skills to provide a secure attachment.

Under-protective parents, on the other hand, build the basis for codependency by not providing their child with enough support. Independence is something that needs to be found gradually, over time. We need to be provided with a safe and secure base as a child in order to feel confident enough to build our own security. Missing this vital step can leave a child feeling very alone and unsafe in the world. Some children with under-protective parents might find that they overcompensate for this feeling by becoming overly autonomous, rejecting any needs for guidance and support. But despite this, the underlying fears and sense of aloneness will be difficult to shake.

Likewise, children who grew up with an alcoholic parent/s can easily find themselves in codependent relationships in later life because the pattern of neglecting their own needs for the needs of another is so familiar.

Like many psychological traits, both positive and negative, codependent tendencies may be rooted in the childhood experience. As children, we form our basis for healthy relationships based on our relationships with parents and other family members. Codependency issues typically develop when someone is raised by parents who are either overprotective or under protective.

Overprotective parents may shield or protect their children from gaining the confidence they need to be independent in the world. In such situations, a child may grow up to be scared of trying new things. For example, a parent may have forbidden you from learning to skateboard for fear of you getting hurt. This seems reasonable and parental protection is a natural response up to a point but can have many negative psychological consequences if it becomes intensely overbearing.

Another form of overprotective parenting can come in the form of coddling to the extent that a child never learns basic life skills. If a child is never taught basic life skills, it makes sensethat they will seek someone to fill those responsibilities in adulthood. To view examples of this type of unhealthy parenting, observe any freshman college dorm. Within the first few weeks of dorm life, it will become apparent who was given the skills they need to begin an independent life. Many college students will find themselves in a difficult situation, having never been taught how to do simple things such as wash their clothes.

On the other side of the parenting spectrum, we see many cases of under-protective parents. These types of parents can help build the foundation for codependency by not providing enough support in development. In a healthy parent-child relationship, we see a solid foundation of confidence that allows a child to build independence at a healthy rate over several years. When this is not the case, a child may end up feeling very alone and unsafe in the world. Many children of under-protective parents may end up overcompensating by becoming very resistant to any guidance or support.

We often see that many children coming from households with parents that have substance use problems may have issues with codependency themselves later in life. This may be due to their familiarity with neglecting their own needs for the needs of another person. In these situations, the parent-child relationship is reversed, and the child is the primary caregiver for their parent. It happens more often than you may think.

Children raised in unhealthy households may have an inherent need to satisfy those around them. They may also seek emotional fulfillment from the satisfaction of other people. As children, we are often at the mercy of our household situation. As adults, we're free to break the cycle of codependency.

Codependency issues often go hand in hand with substance use and other mental health conditions in what is known as a co-occurring disorder.

Although a number of predictors have been proposed for codependency, there is no consensus on the exact causes of the behavioral pattern. Research suggests that the following factors may have a role in developing codependent tendencies:

Codependency is often thought to be a result of living with alcoholic parents or other family members who struggle with substance abuse.

Codependency may begin in childhood, as children often grow up modeling behaviors after a parent who may have been codependent or in a codependent relationship.

Codependency may also be the result of a traumatic event, whether in childhood or adulthood.

A complex relationship between codependency and narcissism has been established, indicating that the two often go hand in hand and even sometimes overlap.

While childhood abuse, traumatic experiences, and exposure to narcissistic behaviors of parents and/or partners seem to play a role, it is difficult to predict codependency on the basis of any of these factors alone.

Codependency is usually rooted in childhood. Often, a child grows up in a home where their emotions are ignored or punished. This emotional neglect can give the child low self-esteem and shame. They may believe their needs are not worth attending to.

Typically, one or more parents are not filling their role as guardians. Their dysfunction could be due to addiction, mental health diagnoses, or other concerns. The child may need to perform tasks that exceed their developmental ability. For example, if a parent is regularly too drunk to fix dinner, a young child may learn to cook, so the family doesn't go hungry.

Often the line between child and adult becomes blurred. If a parent isn't filling their role, a child may become a pseudo-parent for their siblings. They might change a brother's diapers or help a sister finish her homework.

Sometimes the child is expected to care for their own parent. A parent experiencing domestic violence may turn to the child as a confidante. A parent with narcissism may demand the child provide them praise and comfort. These interactions are often called enmeshment.

Since children are not fully grown, filling the role of "adult" can take all their effort. A child may be so focused on keeping the household running that they ignore their own needs. They may associate the caregiving role with feelings of stability and control.

As a child, codependent behaviors can be necessary for survival. In adulthood, the behaviors are not as adaptive. In fact, codependency can prevent a person from developing truly stable relationships.

How to Stop Being Codependent

❖ **Understand what codependency looks like to you**

The first thing you need to do in order to break away and heal from this type of dynamic is to understand what it looks like to you. Which side of the coin are you on?

Do you find that your mood, happiness, or sense of self are defined by your significant other? For example, are you unshakably low on the days your partner, family member, or friend is moody?

Or do you find yourself resorting to dishonest tactics to avoid confrontation with important people in your life for fear of retaliation?

Conversely, maybe you have trouble trusting others – which manifests in a compelling need to control others, and commonly find yourself saying statements like "I need you to do this now."

Or maybe you feel totally responsible for your partner's unhealthy actions – so you find yourself repeatedly bailing them out from unfavorable situations.

Some characteristics of codependent individuals may include:

- eeling responsible for others' actions
- Confusing pity for love – leading to a tendency to love people who are perceived as rescuable
- Automatically inclined to do more than one's own "share" in a relationship

Some potential examples of codependency include:

- You feel guilty asking for your own needs and obligated to do things for others.
- You feel "mean" when you say no, or guilty when asserting yourself.
- You feel anxious about making sure everything is smooth in your relationship or friendship.
- You feel others have control over your life – or, conversely, you've been accused of being a "control freak."
- You actively feel resentful towards others, especially when they take care of themselves.
- You constantly have pangs of FOMO and feel lonely, unloved, and uncared for.

There's no right or wrong – it's a question of determining your own patterns, so you can begin the healing process that's necessary to move past them.

- ❖ **Figure out where your relationship expectations are coming from**

"Until we can detangle these emotions for ourselves, it will be difficult to grow out of a codependent cycle."

"One challenging aspect of recovery from a codependent relationship is pulling back from blaming the other person for the problems,."

More often than not, it's never just one person who's the source of all things wrong with an interpersonal relationship.

We tend to bring our "family ghosts from the past" into our adult relationships. All those past disappointments and resentments can affect how we interact with others.

Until we can detangle these emotions for ourselves, it will be difficult to grow out of a codependent cycle,."

Spend some time meditating and reflecting on what your family's relationship expectations were. For example, what role did your mother play for your father, or what role were you expected to play for your siblings? Understanding where your relationship expectations are coming from can help you identify unhealthy patterns in your current relationships.

Therapy can be a way to dedicate time to understanding these patterns, too. Unpacking expectations from your upbringing (also known as a family of origin) is also the expert realm of psychodynamic and psychoanalytic therapists; consider looking for therapists who take these therapy approaches.

❖ **Establish boundaries for yourself in relationships**

The nature of codependency is such that it tends to blur the lines between where one begins and another ends.

Those healing from codependent relationships may benefit from developing a stronger sense of self.

The following acts can help you develop stronger boundaries:

- o Determine what your core values are. These may include time with family, culture, religion, work, or passion projects. Identifying these, as well as the time you need to allot to them, can help you stay on track with what's important to you. As a result, your needs won't get eclipsed by your partner's values or needs.
- o Let yourself change, rather than trying to change others. Remember, the only adult you're in charge of is yourself – so channel your energy into self-improvement, rather than draining yourself worrying about someone else.
- o Take time to reflect every day. Whether it's sitting in complete silence every night or musing about the day ahead while you're in the shower, turning this into a habit will allow you to grow a deeper connection with yourself.
- o Establishing stronger boundaries can help you say "no" to a friend or partner's requests, or, on the flip side, to understand that just because your partner doesn't need you, 24/7 doesn't mean they don't love you. It can also help you identify how – and when – to walk away from situations that aren't healthy for you.

❖ Resist the urge to fix, control, or save

Often, codependency feeds off a false sense of control. We may think we know what the other person wants – and that it's up to us to help them get it.

While there's nothing wrong with being helpful, doing too much – exhausting our energy in "mind-reading," and trying to remedy situations before they even happen – may lead to a codependent dynamic. It's also easy to get stuck in this type of pattern.

If you're ever stuck in a "fixer," remind yourself: "I can't truly know what the other person wants or needs; only they do." While you can still be compassionate and helpful when someone you love is struggling, you needn't assume to know what someone needs before they ask.

That's not to say you can't be compassionate and helpful when someone you love is struggling. It just means that you needn't assume to know what someone needs before they ask.

❖ Prioritize Your Own Growth

At the end of the day, relationships are meant to complement your already awesome life – not be your entire life.

"It can help to identify what your unspoken expectations might have been in the relationship, and then to explore where those expectations came from."

Is there something you were trying to get from the partner, family member, or friend in question that would be better off coming from you instead?

Taking a break from patterns of codependency allows you to channel that time and energy back into yourself. Try the following acts to foster self-growth:

Practice saying "no" to yourself. Practice makes perfect, even if it's during alone time. Say "no, thank you!" out loud if you find yourself pulled into social media or habits you're looking to break away from.

Schedule time into your calendar to pursue a hobby or passion project you love every week.

Actively listen to your self-talk. The next time you catch yourself talking down to yourself, turn that negative thinking into something more positive.

Working with a therapist can help you figure out where your codependent tendencies come from and determine techniques to overcome and heal.

❖ **First, separate showing support from codependence.**

The line between healthy, supportive behaviors and codependent ones can sometimes be a bit blurry. After all, it's normal to want to help your partner, especially if they're having a tough time.

But codependent behavior is a way to direct or control someone else's behavior or mood, "You're jumping into the driver's seat of their life instead of remaining a passenger.

It might not be your intention to control them, but over time, your partner may come to depend on your help and do less for themselves. In turn, you might feel a sense of fulfillment or purpose from the sacrifices you make for your partner.

Other key signs of codependency might include:

- o Preoccupation with your partner's behavior or well-being
- o Worrying more about your partner's behavior than they do
- o A mood that depends on how your partner feels or acts

The sooner you notice the signs of a codependent relationship, the easier it will be to work through them. And if you recognize that *you're* the codependent partner, you'll need to do some work on yourself:

- o Doing some activities by yourself, like going to the beach or to the movies
- o Thinking about all the things that bring you joy, independent of your partner
- o Prioritizing self-care
- o Reflecting on any trauma you've experienced
- o Speaking with a therapist

As a couple, you can work through codependency, but it will take a lot of communication and honesty from both parties about what's been going on in the relationship. "Establish boundaries with the other person, and don't be guided by guilt,." If communicating about this topic is challenging, attending therapy together may help. There's also a 12-step group called Codependents Anonymous, similar to

Alcoholics Anonymous, which can help people break out of their codependent habits.

If the codependent relationship has gone on for too long, it may be beyond repair. It'll be more complicated if you have a family together because the decision will affect your children, but it depends on you and your partner's willingness to build a healthier relationship. "If you don't have children together, you should leave when there is no cooperation or commitment from the other person to change,."

Changing goes both ways, even if you're the one that's codependent. "Your partner needs to be prepared to work through this with you and address how their past may have fed into this dynamic,." Typically, it takes therapy and a commitment to solo work from both halves of the codependent relationship to make it work.

❖ Identify patterns in your life.

Once you've got a handle on what codependency actually looks like, take a step back and try to identify any recurring patterns in your current and past relationships.

Codependent behaviors are typically rooted in childhood. Patterns you learn from your parents and repeat in relationships usually play out again and again until you put a stop to them. But it's hard to break a pattern before you notice it.

Do you have a tendency to gravitate toward people who need a lot of help? Do you have a hard time asking your partner for help?

Codependent people tend to rely on validation from others instead of self-validation. These tendencies toward self-sacrifice might help you feel closer to your partner. When you aren't doing things for them, you might feel aimless, uncomfortable, or experience lower self-esteem.

Simply acknowledging these patterns is key to overcoming them.

❖ Learn what healthy love looks like

Not all unhealthy relationships are codependent, but all codependent relationships are generally unhealthy.

This doesn't mean codependent relationships are doomed. It's just going to take some work to get things back on track. One of the first steps in doing so is simply learning what a healthy, non-codependent relationship looks like.

"Healthy love involves a cycle of comfort and contentment," "while toxic love involves a cycle of pain and despair."

A few more signs of healthy love:

- o Partners trust themselves and each other
- o Both partners feel secure in their own self-worth
- o Partners can compromise

In a healthy relationship, your partner should care about your feelings, and you should feel safe to communicate your emotions and needs. You should also feel able to voice an opinion that differs from your partner's or say no to something that conflicts with your own needs.

❖ Set boundaries for yourself

A boundary is a limit you set around things you aren't comfortable with. They're not always easy to set or stick to, especially if you're dealing with long-standing codependency. You might be so accustomed to making others comfortable that you have a hard time considering your own limits.

It might take some practice before you can firmly and repeatedly honor your own boundaries, but these tips can help:

Listen with empathy, but stop there. Unless you're involved with the problem, don't offer solutions or try to fix it for them.

Practice polite refusals. Try "I'm sorry, but I'm not free at the moment" or "I'd rather not tonight, but maybe another time."

Question yourself. Before you do something, ask yourself the following questions:

- o Why am I doing this?
- o Do I want to, or do I feel I have to?
- o Will this drain any of my resources?
- o Will I still have the energy to meet my own needs?
- ❖ **Remember, you can only control your own actions**.

Trying to control someone else's actions generally don't work out. But if you feel validated by your ability to support and care for your partner, failing at this can make you feel pretty miserable.

Their lack of change might frustrate you. You might feel resentful or disappointed that your helpful efforts had little effect. These emotions can either leave you feeling worthless or more determined to try even harder and begin the cycle again.

How can you stop this pattern?

Remind yourself you can only control yourself. You have a responsibility to manage your own behaviors and reactions. You aren't responsible for your partner's behavior or anyone else's.

Giving up control involves accepting uncertainty. No one knows what the future holds. This can be scary, especially if fears of being alone or losing your relationship contribute to codependent behaviors. But the healthier your relationship is, the more likely it is to last.

❖ Offer healthy support

There's nothing wrong with wanting to help your partner, but there are ways to do so without sacrificing your own needs.

Healthy support might involve:

- o Talking about problems to get new perspectives
- o Listening to your partner's troubles or worries
- o Discussing possible solutions with them, rather than for them
- o Offering suggestions or advice when asked, then stepping back to let them make their own decision
- o Offering compassion and acceptance

Remember, you can show love for your partner by spending time with them and being there for them without trying to manage or direct their behavior. Partners should value each other for who they are, not what they do for each other.

❖ Have a spiritual practice

Love yourself by spending time alone. Whether or not you believe in God, spiritual practice is an excellent means of creating a deeper relationship with yourself. What better way to honor you than by setting aside some quiet time each day.

Spiritual practice doesn't require religious beliefs. Your intention may simply be to find a centered, calm place to access inner guidance, to develop reverence for life, or to experience harmony with yourself and others. Listening and finding your truth gives you greater confidence, clarity, and peace. It helps you let go of control and not react, despite what's happening around you.

❖ Practice valuing yourself

Codependency and low self-esteem are often linked. If you link your self-worth to your ability to care for others, developing a sense of self-worth that doesn't depend on your relationships with others can prove challenging.

But increased self-worth can increase your confidence, happiness, and self-esteem. All of this can make it easier for you to express your needs and set boundaries, both of which are key to overcoming codependency.

Learning to value yourself takes time. These tips can set you on the right path:

1) Spend time with people who treat you well. It's not always easy to leave a relationship, even when you're ready to move on. In the meantime, surround yourself with positive people who value you and offer acceptance and support. Limit your time with people who drain your energy and say or do things that make you feel bad about yourself.

2) Do things you enjoy. Maybe the time you've spent looking after others has kept you from hobbies or other interests. Try setting aside some time each day to do things that make you happy, whether it's reading a book or taking a walk.

3) Take care of your health. Caring for your body can help your emotional well-being improve, too. Make sure you're eating regularly and getting enough sleep each night. These are essential needs that you deserve to have met.

4) Let go of negative self-talk. If you tend to criticize yourself, challenge and reframe these negative thought patterns to affirm yourself instead. Instead of "I'm no good," for example, tell yourself, "I'm trying my best."

❖ **Identify your own needs.**

Remember, codependent patterns often begin in childhood. It may have been a long time since you stopped to think about your own needs and desires.

Ask yourself what you want from life, independentof anyone else's desires. Do you want a relationship? A family? A specific type of job? To live elsewhere? Try journaling about whatever these questions bring up.

Trying new activities can help. If you aren't sure what you enjoy, try things that interest you. You might find you have a talent or skill you never knew about.

This isn't a quick process. It may take weeks, months, or even years to develop concrete ideas about what you really need and want. But that's OK. The important part is that you're thinking about it.

❖ Receive support

Love yourself by asking for and receiving help. Human beings are social animals and need each other. When you're lonely, confused, anxious, overwhelmed, or in the dumps, reaching out is a way of giving to yourself. Sometimes, turning to God brings comfort and guidance. Other times, your emotions take over, and you're unable to think or calm yourself. That's when you need others.

There are times when everyone needs support. When problems persist and don't go away on their own, you require more than friends can offer. Unfortunately, some people believe that asking for and receiving help are signs of weakness. If you're used to helping others, you probably don't feel worthy of or comfortable receiving help.

Changing that pattern is growth. Whether it's going to a meeting or seeking professional counseling, getting support isn't an indulgence or a character flaw. In fact, it takes self-honesty to know your limits and humility and courage toask for help. Doing soallows others to giveand feel close to you. Appreciating their love and support is human and healthy.

❖ Meet your needs

Love yourself by attending to your needs. If you've been tending the needs of others but neglecting your own, it's time to turn that around and put yourself first. The reverse also happens — you expect others to fill needs that are your responsibility.

Be sure to address your basic physical needs, such as healthy food, rest, exercise, and medical and dental checkups. Give special attention to needs you may be overlooking. When you're lonely, sad, angry, afraid, overwhelmed, confused, tired, or feeling like a victim, ask yourself what you need. If you're depressed, you may have been avoiding and neglecting yourself for a long time.

Some needs are met by others, such as needs for intimacy and friendship. It's your obligation to speak up and ask for what you need and want. Expecting others to read your mind leads to resentment and conflict.

❖ **Have fun**

ove yourself by planning pleasure, recreation, and hobbies. These are needs, too. Focusing on a problem often makes it worse. Without balance, pain can turn into self-pity and become a wayof life. There are also people who take themselves tooseriously. They develop tunnel vision when it comes to work and problems. For them, living is a struggle, a competition, or a test of enduranceand achievement.

You may have forgotten how to laugh and enjoy yourself, which is important in maintaining balance in your body's chemistry and in your life. Life isn't meant to be a burden but to be enjoyed. Celebrate it by making time to relax, play, and be creative — activities that are rejuvenating and bring you into the present.

Sometimes, when you take a break and have fun — even for a short time — your worries magically dissolve, and you gain a new perspective on a problem. Pleasure restores your energy and sense of well-being, which not only nourishes your soul but alsoenhances theproductivityand quality of your work.

❖ Protect yourself

Love yourself by protecting yourself from physical, mental, and emotional abuse. Loving someone doesn't mean you have to accept insulting or -demeaning words or behavior. If you think you're being abused, don't waste your energy or risk your safety trying to change the abuser, explaining your position, or proving your innocence. It doesn't matter.

You didn't cause, nor are you responsible for, other peoples' words or behavior, but you do have a responsibility to protect yourself and your children. You have a choice to speak up, set limits, disengage from the conversation, leave the room, get professional help, call the police when there's violence, or end the relationship.

❖ Accept yourself

Love yourself as the unique individual you are, including your appearance, feelings, thoughts, and addictions. You don't have to earn respect or prove anything. You're deserving of love and respect as a human being with flaws and failures. Notice if you're trying to change for someone else's validation. Instead, remind yourself that being yourself is more important. When you practice self-acceptance, you stop worrying about what others think and can be more authentic and spontaneous.

Becoming and accepting yourself takes time. Forcing change with constant self-evaluation and selfjudgment keeps you stuck, but self-acceptanceallows change to happen with little effort. When you slipor make mistakes, remember that self-criticism compounds them. It's much moreproductive to forgiveyourself and focus on your behavior in the present.

❖ Gentle yourself

Love yourself with gentleness and compassion. Modulate your inner voice so that it's calm and kind. When you're afraid or in pain, blaming yourself or thinking there's something wrong with you makes matters worse. When you're tempted to ignore your feelings and distract yourself with more activity, obsessions, or addictive behavior, practice just being with yourself.

Be the one who is there for you with gentleness and compassion in your anxiety, sorrow, hopelessness, anger, and terror. The child within you needs you. Comfort yourself with all the tenderness you would like a crying child or wounded animal. Listen, forgive, and embrace your full humanness. Develop the trust that you can count on yourself.

❖ Encourage yourself

Love yourself with encouragement and enthusiasm. Transform your inner critic into a positive coach. Get in the habit of finding things you do well and acknowledging them. Don't wait for others to appreciate and compliment you. Appreciate and compliment yourself.

In fact, repeat praise over and over. Instead of taking your good qualities for granted, notice them, and give yourself credit. Look for small things you do right and well. How good it feels hearing encouragement! Stop doubting yourself, and pay attention to every small sign of progress toward your goals. Tell yourself you can make it — you can do whatever you desire. When you love yourself with encouragement, watch your self-confidence and success grow:

❖ Express yourself

Love yourself by expressing yourself. Your self has been hidden too long. Healing shame requires that you risk being seen. Commit to stop hiding and honor yourself by communicating your feelings, opinions, thoughts, and needs. You have a right to think and feel what you do without explanation,or justification. Your self-respect and the respect you receive from others will grow.

Self-expression alsoincludesyour creativity. Expressyourself in music, writing, design, art, cooking, crafts, dance, or wherever your creativity leads you. Tell your inner Critic you're creating for fun and not to bother you.

❖ Pursue your passions

Love yourself by following your passions. Only you hold the keys to your happiness. Talking yourself out of pursuing your desires leads to discontent and regret. Even if your desires are impractical or unprofitable, don't allow those obstacles to discourage you.

Every day, take one small step toward realizing your goals or doing something that excites you. If you're uncertain about your passions, pay attention to what stimulates you. Listen to what calls to you, follow your inspiration, and take risks to experience the fullness of who you are.

If you're depressed or overwhelmed, it can be hard to think about positive goals. For now, make your recovery your number-oneobjective. In time, you will have moreenergy and motivation about the future and your desires. Be patient. Goals or a specific direction eventually emerge.

❖ Consider therapy

Codependent traits can become so entrenched in personality and behavior that you might have a hard time recognizing them on your own. Even when you do notice them, codependency can be tough to overcome solo.

If you're working to overcome codependency, seek help from a therapist who has experience working with recovery from this complicated issue.

They can help you:

- o Identify and take steps to address patterns of codependent behavior
- o Work on increasing self-esteem
- o Explore what you want from life
- o Reframe and challenge negative thought patterns

"Continuing to place your focus outside of yourself puts you into a position of powerlessness,." Over time, this can contribute to feelings of hopelessness and helplessness, which can contribute to depression.

Codependency is a complex issue, but with a little work, you can overcome it and start building more balanced relationships that serve your needs, too.

Some individuals are able to overcome codependency on their own. Learning about what it means to be codependent and the harm it causes can be enough for some individuals to change their behavior. Some steps you can take to overcome codependence include:

Look for signs of a healthy relationship. In order to break out of codependent patterns, you need to first understand what a healthy, loving relationship looks like. Signs of a healthy relationship include making time for each other, maintaining independence, being honest and open, showing affection, and having equality.

They have healthy boundaries. People with good relationships are supportive of each other, but they also respect each other's boundaries. A boundary is a limit that establishes what you are willing and unwilling to accept in a relationship. Spend some time thinking about what is acceptable to you. Work on listening to the other person, but don't allow their problems to consume your life. Practice finding ways to decline requests that step over your boundaries.

❖ Set limits, then work on enforcing them.

Take care of yourself. People who are in codependent relationships often have low self-esteem. In order to stop being codependent, you need to start by valuing yourself. Learn more about the things that make you happy and the kind of life that you want to live. Spend time doing the things that you love to do. Work on overcoming negative self-talk and replace self-defeating thoughts with more positive, realistic ones. Also, be sure that you are taking care of your health by getting the food, rest, and self-care that you need for your emotional well-being.

Some people learn about their codependent tendencies through books or articles. Others stop being codependent when they experience environmental changes, such as when a partner becomes sober, or they get a new job that requires them to stop care-taking.

It is important for both partners to see a therapist and undergo treatment when codependency is involved. One spouse may battle addiction and the other codependency, for example, and both will need to work through the negative and destructive emotions and patterns of behavior that are attached to each issue.

Spouses, or partners, will need to learn how not to enable a loved one who suffers from addiction. Families and spouses are encouraged to attend some form of treatment and therapy that offers help for codependency with a loved one who is battling addiction while they are also in a treatment program.

Codependency can hamper addiction treatment and recovery if it isn't addressed and managed at the same time as the addiction issue. Addiction treatment programs often offer support and educational programs for families and loved ones of those in treatment to help them better understand the disease of addiction and their own role in recovery going forward. With therapeutic intervention, a codependent relationship may be improved, and both partners may be able to recognize the dysfunctions within the relationship and move forward in a healthier manner.

Not all codependent relationships may be saved, however, as both members need to invest in change and commit to getting necessary help. Abuse often accompanies codependence, and this cannot be tolerated. Both partners in a codependent relationship will need to commit to change and work together toward recovery in order for the relationship to be salvaged.

A few things can help toward forming a positive, balanced relationship:

- People in codependent relationships may need to take small steps toward some separation in the relationship. They may need to find a hobby or activity they enjoy outside of the relationship.
- A codependent person should try to spend time with supportive family members or friends.
- The enabler must decide that they are not helping their codependent partner by allowing them to make extreme sacrifices.
- Individual or group therapy is very helpful for people who are in codependent relationships. An expert can help them find ways to acknowledge and express their feelings that may have been buried since childhood.

- People who were abused will need to recognize past abuse and start to feel their own needs and emotions again.
- Finally, both parties in a codependent relationship must learn to acknowledge specific patterns of behavior, such as "needing to be needed" and expecting the other person to center their life around them.

These steps are not easy to do but are well worth the effort to help both parties discover how to be in a balanced, two-sided relationship.

Codependency often requires professional treatment, however. It can be treated with talk therapy. Research shows that several types of therapy treatments can be effective in improving the quality of one's life and learning how to stop being codependent.

❖ Group Therapy

There areseveralgroup interventions that may be effective for codependency. The group dynamic gives individuals an opportunity to form healthier relationships in an appropriate space. Group therapy often involves giving positive feedback and holding individuals accountable.

Group therapy methods may vary. Some involve cognitive behavioral therapy, where members learn specific skill-building strategies.

Other codependency groups follow the 12-step model. Similar to the way other 12-step groups are run, individuals learn about their relationship addiction. Goals may include increasing self-awareness, self-esteem, and the expression of feelings.

❖ Family Therapy

Family therapy targets dysfunctional family dynamics. Family members learn how to recognize their dysfunctional patterns so they can learn how to improve their relationships.

Improved communication is often a key goal of family therapy. Issues that have never before been discussed in the family may be raised in therapy. Sometimes, one individual creates a change (such as getting sober or encouraging someone to be more independent), and it can change the entire family dynamic.

❖ Cognitive Therapy

Cognitive therapy can target the thoughts that contribute to unhealthy relationship patterns. For example, an individual who thinks, "I can't stand being alone," is likely to go to great lengths to maintain the relationship, even when it's not healthy to do so. Therapy sessions might focus on learning how to tolerate uncomfortable emotions and changing irrational thoughts.

The goal is likely to create positive behavior changes and allow the other individual to accept more personal responsibility for their own actions.

Treatment may delve into a person's childhood since most codependent individuals are patterning their relationships after ones they grew up seeing. Therapy may assist someone in getting in touch with their emotions and helping them experience a wide range of feelings again.

CODEPENDENCY AND ADDICTION

Codependency often goes hand in hand with addiction, as spouses or partners of someone battling addiction may regularly enable them to continue problematic drinking or drug-using behaviors, making excuses for them and helping them to cover it up. A codependent spouse often enables the user by making excuses for them, cleaning up their messes, and taking care of them when they are intoxicated or sobering up.

Someone who suffers from codependency needs to be needed and goes out of their way to help their partner or loved one regardless of any personal consequences. This is, of course, unhealthy and does not serve either person in the relationship as it allows the same mistakes and unhealthy behaviors to be perpetuated and ignored.

Codependency may arise when someone is in a relationship with a person who has an addiction. The partner may abuse substances, or they may have an addiction to gambling or shopping.

Addiction impairs judgment and critical thinking skills. This makes it very difficult for someone with a substance use disorder to see that they need help. When you go out of your way to prevent your partner from experiencing the consequences of substance abuse, you make it less likely that they will acknowledge that a problem exists.

Loving someone with a substance use disorder can also cause your codependent tendencies to spiral out of control. When your partner is behaving erratically due to drug or alcohol abuse, it's easy to resort to using codependent behavior in your fight to maintain a sense of control over chaotic surroundings. This creates a vicious cycle that traps both of you in a dysfunctional and unhealthy relationship.

The person with codependency may take on a "caretaker" role for their partner. The partner may rely on the caretaker to handle finances or household chores. If the addiction causes issues outside the relationship, the caretaker may cover for their partner. For example, someone who abuses alcohol may skip work. A codependent person may call the partner's boss on their behalf and claim their partner is ill.

The caretaker often cares for their partner out of a sincere desire to help. Yet, their behavior often enables their partner to continue the addiction. When the caretaker "saves" the partner from consequences, the partner often loses motivation to change. They may not seek the professional rehab they need. Without help, the addiction may get worse.

And if one partner in your relationship has an addiction, it's much more likely to become codependent. One partner's addiction to alcohol or drugs can take a toll on both partners and can cause more imbalances in the relationship. "So can addiction to money, ego, power, lying, or love and sex,." The person with the addiction can neglect his or her partner in the process, while the other may feel the need to give more to that person out of fear, guilt, or habit, according to Beattie.

Addiction and codependency are, unfortunately, observed on a regular basis. Addiction is a chronic disease that affects brain function. It causes the sufferer to prioritize substance abuse higher than logic or reason dictates. Sadly, it's all too easy for spouses, parents, or any other family members to fall into the cycle of codependent behavior.

For some reason, perhaps as a result of the stigma attached to addiction, lots of people try to sweep substance use disorders under the rug. Don't attempt to deal with addiction — which is a diagnosable mental health disorder — in the family. Seek professional help for the codependent person and an addiction recovery program at rehab for the person engaging in drug or alcohol abuse.

That said, the caretaker is not to blame for the other person's addiction. While codependency can contribute to someone refusing treatment, it is not the only cause. Barring a safety crisis, someone cannot force others into rehabilitation.

This relationship can also harm the caretaker. The codependent person often throws their own needs to the side to care for the partner. Their codependent habits can worsen with time. They are unlikely to seek treatment for their own mental health concerns.

A codependent person may appear selfless and strong; however, these types of relationships are highly dysfunctional and unhealthy. Codependent relationships and maladaptive behaviors are unlikely to improve on their own. In fact, they will likely get worse over time, Psych Central warns. With treatment that targets these behaviors along with other mental health problems, codependency is reversible, and relationships may be salvageable.

How does a codependent relationship develop?

Codependency is a learned behavior that usually stems from past behavioral patterns and emotional difficulties. It was once thought to be a result of living with an alcoholic parent.

Codependency can result from a range of situations.

✦ Damaging parental relationships

People who are codependent as adults often had problems with their parental relationship as a child or teenager.

They may have been taught that their own needs were less important than their parent's needs or not important at all.

In these types of families, the child may be taught to focus on the parent's needs and to never think of themselves.

Needy parents may teach their children that children are selfish or greedy if they want anything for themselves.

As a result, the child learns to ignore their own needs and thinks only of what they can do for others at all times.

In these situations, one of the parents may have:

- o An addiction problem with alcohol or drugs
- o A lack of maturity and emotional development, resulting in their own self-centered needs

These situations cause gaps in emotional development in the child, leading them to seek out codependent relationships later.

⥚ Living with a mentally or physically ill family member

Codependency may also result from caring for a person who is chronically ill. Being in the role of caregiver, especially at a young age, may result in the young person neglecting their own needs and developing a habit of only helping others.

A person's self-worth may form around being needed by another person and receiving nothing in return.

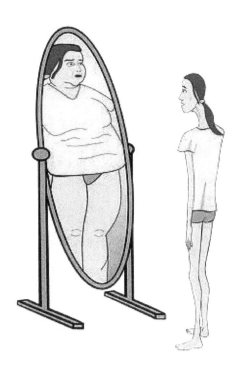

Many people who live with an ill family member do not develop codependency. But, it can happen in these types of family environments, particularly if the parent or primary caretaker in the family displays the dysfunctional behaviors listed above.

✦ Abusive families

Physical, emotional, and sexual abuse can cause psychological problems that last years or even an entire lifetime. One of the many issues that can arise from past abuse is codependency.

A child or teenager who is abused will learn to repress their feelings as a defense mechanism against the pain of abuse.

As an adult, this learned behavior results in caring only about another's feelings and not acknowledging their own needs.

Sometimes a person who is abused will seek out abusive relationships later because they are only familiar with this type of relationship. This often manifests in codependent relationships.

Usually, codependent relationships don't just happen out of nowhere and often are a projection of past relationships you've had, especially with family members.

"Codependency usually develops from parent-child relations that influence the child to put their parents' or family's needs before their own.

Sometimes, people who are more inclined to slide into a codependent relationship have had a toxic relationship with a parent or family member; this doesn't necessarily mean that one party had an intention of controlling the other person, but it can happen, especially if a parent has been ill, has struggled with substance abuse, or has been emotionally unstable. Codependency can also happen when a person is such a devoted caregiver for someone else that they neglect their own needs. While caregiving can inherently be a beautiful, unselfish act, it can turn unhealthy. "It is imperative to understand that a relationship wrapped in the need for another person, and the need to be needed, is not healthy,."

People might also have personality traits that make them more inclined to develop a codependent relationship with another person. For example, if you are always apologizing, leading every text and email with "sorry!," even for mundane things, it could be a sign of a codependent trait. "This can signal a need to know that people are not mad at you,."

Along with that, if you have trouble expressing exactly what you want in a relationship (this can be something as simple as where you want to pick up dinner or a bigger decision like where you want to move with your partner), it can be problematic in the long run. Codependent relationships thrive on one person "going along with" the other person's wishes, and adapting to that person's will can weigh on you over time.

Codependence vs. dependence

It is important to know the difference between depending on another person — which can be a positive and desirable trait — and codependency, which is harmful.

The following are some examples that illustrate the difference:

Dependent: Two people rely on each other for support and love. Both find value in the relationship.

Codependent: The codependent person feels worthless unless they are needed by — and making drastic sacrifices for — the enabler. The enabler gets satisfaction from getting every need met by the other person.

The codependent is only happy when making extreme sacrifices for their partner. They feel they must be needed by this other person to have any purpose.

Dependent: Both parties make their relationship a priority but can find joy in outside interests, other friends, and hobbies.

Codependent: The codependent has no personal identity, interests, or values outside of their codependent relationship.

Dependent: Both people can express their emotions and needs and find ways to make the relationship beneficial for both of them.

Codependent: One person feels that their desires and needs are unimportant and will not express them. They may have difficulty recognizing their own feelings or needs at all.

Dependent: The relationship is a priority for both people, but happiness can be found in other interests, friends, and pastimes. Both people in a relationship can express their concerns and needs openly. Reliance on each other is mutual, and both individuals value their relationship highly.

Codependent: The relationship is one-sided in caring for the interests of one person in the relationship. Happiness is dependent on caring for the other person, often including sacrifices at the expense of the codependent person. Outside interests are severely limited as time and energy are focused on caring for the other person. The expression of personal needs and wants are considered unimportant or are not taken into consideration at all.

One or both parties can be codependent. A codependent person will neglect other important areas of their life to please their partner. Their extreme dedication to this one person may cause damage to:

o   Other relationships

- Their career
- Their everyday responsibilities

The enabler's role is also dysfunctional. A person who relies upon a codependent does not learn how to have an equal, two-sided relationship and often comes to rely upon another person's sacrifices and neediness.

Styles of Codependent Relationships

Experts used to think of Codependency is a problem that goes along with alcoholism. Nowadays, we know that it can happen in a wider variety of situations. There's no way to list every type of codependent relationship; after all, every situation is unique, but here are some of the most common types of Codependency:

> **Addict + Caretaker**

However, addicts of all kinds attract codependent partners. It doesn't matter if the problem is alcohol, drugs, gambling, shopping, or whatever else. What matters is that all addicts tend to behave irresponsibly, destructively, and selfishly which makes them very, very difficult people to live with. Their partners (platonic or otherwise) fall into the Codependent Caretaker role by cleaning up their messes and providing them with what they need to continue on with their harmful behavior.

This relationship boosts the self-esteem of the caretaker, as it makes them feel needed and important. You may hear this kind of codependent person say things like, "I'm the responsible one in this relationship."

> **Parent + Child**

Perhaps one of the most troubling forms of codependency occurs between parent and child because it inhibits a young person's emotional development. Typically, the parent becomes emotionally dependent on their role as a caretaker to their naturally needy young children. It's quite normal for all parents to gain a feeling of pride in their familial role. However, codependent parents behave in a way to prolong the 'needy state' of their children, unnaturally prolonging their role as caretakers. They will prevent their kids from growing up into independent adults so that they forever rely on their parents for everything.

You can imagine how difficult it is for the child to break free from this relationship since it formed a major part of their development.

You might hear a codependent parent complain about their child's lack of independence. However, their behavior will contradict that. You will see them continue to spoil and encourage their adult children to rely on them.

> ### Dysfunctional Adult + Enabler

When we shirk responsibilities and fail to meet life's basic demands, the universe responds with a swift kick to the behind. Not paying bills and skimping on self-care gets us into trouble, which usually 'trains' us to be more responsible. Messing up once or twice is usually enough for us to learn to get our acts together as adults. However, in some cases, dysfunctional adults find a partner willing to take over when they give up. This partner is an Enabler because their overly helpful behavior allows the dysfunctional person to continue on their path of self-neglect. Ironically, the enabler is doing much more damage with kindness than they realize. A stern, realistic influence is what the dysfunctional person really needs.

You might hear the enabler say things like: "I'm the sane one," or "I don't know what (s)he would do without me."

What is a Dysfunctional Family and How Does it Lead to Co-dependency?

A dysfunctional family is one in which members suffer from fear, anger, pain, or shame that is ignored or denied. Underlying problems may include any of the following:

- An addiction by a family member to drugs, alcohol, relationships, work, food, sex, or gambling.
- The existence of physical, emotional, or sexual abuse.
- The presence of a family member suffering from a chronic mental or physical illness.

Dysfunctional families do not acknowledge that problems exist. They don't talk about them or confront them. As a result, family members learn to repress emotions and disregard their own needs. They become "survivors." They develop behaviors that help them deny, ignore, or avoid difficult emotions. They detach themselves. They don't talk. They don't touch. They don't confront. They don't feel. They don't trust. The identity and emotional development of the members of a dysfunctional family are often inhibited.

Attention and energy focus on the family member who is ill or addicted. The co-dependent person typically sacrifices his or her needs to take care of a person who is sick. When co-dependents place other people's health, welfare, and safety before their own, they can lose contact with their own needs, desires, and sense of self.

The co-dependent relationship in the family between the child and parent can be very serious because what children experiences in the family usually sets the tone for the rest of their lives.

When the child manages to enter college, he or she will still carry various issues into adulthood as a result of growing up in a dysfunctional family. For instance, most adult children who grew up to codependent parents always question their judgment and frequently check their decision with others. This lack of confidence will deter the student from taking any leadership position while in college and even lead to an unsuccessful career.

Also, it is common for children of co-dependent parents to have unstable relationships. The co-dependency that they often adapt from their parents makes them feel responsible for everyone who needs help. They are mostly focused on everyone's else need but their own, which deters them from figuring out what their want and their goals in life.

Many dysfunctional families look healthy on the outside, but the internal dynamics revolve around a family member's addiction, abuse, illness, or trauma. Other families are dysfunctional due to rigid control or lack of empathy and acceptance that can cause children to become codependent. The strongest predictor of codependency has codependent parents.

Codependency usually starts when you feel emotionally abandoned. In response, you repress feelings, needs, observations, and thoughts. You learn to numb your hurt, distrust your parents, and become self-sufficient. To cope and be accepted, you hide behind a false personality and/or develop compulsive behaviors to cope. The following are symptoms, but not all are necessary for a family to be dysfunctional. Families with drug addiction or abuse usually have more of the symptoms.

Dysfunctional families are closed to varying degrees. Some won't allow differing or new ideas to be discussed among members or with outsiders. They may not welcome guests or friendships with those of another race or religion. Remember Archie Bunker of All in the Family. He was autocratic and intolerant of opposing views.

Some families are isolated and don't interact with the community. Others do, but appearances are everything. The family may be respected in the community but hides the truth. Talking about the family to others is considered disloyal. At the bottom are shame and fear of dissimilar ideas.

Family problems and crises, such as a member's absence, illness, or addiction, never get talked about. Parents think that if they act normal and pretend the problem doesn't exist, maybe it'll go away, or children won't notice or be harmed. However, this pretense makes you doubt your perceptions because what you see and know aren't acknowledged by authority figures.

You learn not to question or trust your parents nor trust your perceptions, feelings, or yourself, even as an adult. Denial conveys to children that they can't talk about something frightening — even to each other. Sadly, frightened children who share the same bedroom and overhear their parents fighting nonetheless live in silent fear because they can't talk about their pain with each other.

Ask yourself these questions:

- o What truths were dismissed or ignored in your fmily?
- o How did your parents do that?
- o How did it affect you?

Denial breeds secrets. Some families hide a shameful truth for generations — whether it's addiction, violence, criminal activity, sexual issues, or mental illness. That shame is felt by the children — even when they don't know the secret. If you know the secret but can't ask questions or talk about it, you feel different, damaged, or ashamed.

Some of the symptoms that are likely to create dysfunction are described below,

1. Denial. Denial is a way to ignore or pretend that a painful reality doesn't exist. Parents try to act normal amidst family problems and crises – such as a parent's absence, illness, or alcoholism. It never gets talked about, nor the problem solved. This makes children doubt their perceptions and sends a message that they can't talk about something strange and frightening – even to each other.

2. A Closed System. A closed family, unlike G.E., won't allow differing or new ideas to be discussed among members or with outsiders. Members aren't allowed to talk about the family to others and might not allow guests from another race or religion. Some families are isolated and don't interact with the community. Others do, but appearances are everything, and the truth about the family isn't shared. At the bottom are fears of dissimilar ideas and shame.

3. Secrets. Some secrets are kept for generations about a family shame – whether addiction, violence, criminal activity, sexual issues, or mental illness. The shame is felt by children – even when they don't know the secret.

4. Dysfunctional Communication. This can take many forms – from an absence of communication to verbal abuse. Talking is not the same as functional communication, which involves listening, respect, assertiveness, and understanding. In dysfunctional families, communication is neither assertive nor open. People don't listen, and verbal abuse predominates. (See my blogs "Six Keys to Assertive Communication" and "Emotional Abuse – Beneath Your Radar.") Children are afraid to express their thoughts and feelings and are often blamed, shamed, or scolded for self-expression. They are told directly or indirectly not to feel what they feel and maybe labeled a sissy, bad, dumb, lazy, or selfish. They learn not to question their parents and not to trust their perceptions and feelings.

5. Rigid Rules. In some families where there is physical or mental illness, parents are too lax or irresponsible, children lack guidance, and they don't feel safe and cared for. Generally, however, there are restrictive and sometimes arbitrary rules. Many are unspoken. There's no room for mistakes. Some parents take over decisions that children should make and control their hobbies, school courses, friends, and dress. Natural independence is seen as disloyalty and abandonment. They prohibit talking about things deemed "inappropriate," such as sex, death, the holocaust, grandpa's limp, or that father was married before. Some families have rules restricting the expression of anger, exuberance, or crying. When feelings can't be expressed, children learn self-control and become overly controlled or controlling adults, all contributing to low self-esteem.

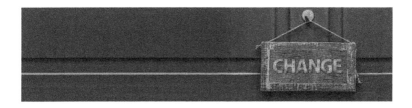

6. Arbitrariness and Inconsistency. What are worse than rigid rules are arbitrary and inconsistent rules. Children never know when they'll be punished. Rules that don't make sense are unjust. This is cruel and breeds learned helplessness and rage that can never be expressed. Children are in constant fear, walk on eggshells, and feel hopeless and resentful because of the unpredictability and unfairness. Their sense of worth and dignity is violated. They lose respect and trust in their parents and authority in general because they're forced to comply; some act out with rebellious or delinquent behavior by doing poorly in school or by using drugs.

7. Role Confusion. This happens when a parent is emotionally or physically absent or is irresponsible, and a child takes on parental responsibilities or becomes a companion or confidante to the other parent. This is frequently the case after a divorce,but also happens in intact families where parents lack intimacy. This is age-inappropriate and damaging to the child psychologically, who must now act like a little adult, repress his or her needs and feelings, and may feel that he or she is betraying the other parent.

8. Unpredictability. People feel safe when family life is predictable. If children never know what mood Mom or Dad will be in, they can't be spontaneous and are always anxious. Even worse is chaos, where the family is in constant crisis, often due to addiction, mental illness, or sexual, physical, or emotional abuse. Instead of a safe haven, the family becomes a war zone to escape. Children may take develop somatic complaints, like headaches and stomach aches.

9. Inability to Problem-Solve. Resolving problems and conflicts is key to a smooth-running organization. But in dysfunctional families, children and parents are blamed repeatedly for the same thing, and there are constant arguments or silent walls of resentment. Nothing gets resolved.

Healthy families are safe because open self-expression is encouraged without judgment or retaliation. Love is shown not only in words but in empathic, nurturing, and supportive behavior. Each member, down to the youngest, is treated as a valued, respected member. Feedback is allowed, and there's a sense of equality, even if parents have the final veto. Parents act responsibly and are accountable for their commitments, and hold children accountable for theirs. They correct and punish misbehavior but don't blame their children or attack their character. Mistakes are allowed and forgiven, and parents acknowledge their own shortcomings. They encourage and guide their children and respect their privacy and physical and emotional boundaries. These ingredients build self-esteem, trust, and integrity.

CONCLUSION

Codependency is not your fault. You didn't cause it. You became codependent as a way to adapt to an unhealthy childhood. Your primary caregivers were not healthy, so your codependent traits developed as survival mechanisms ~ survival adaptations.

As an adult, however, codependency traits cause you problems and get in the way of you having a happy, healthy relationship with your Self and others. So, although you did not cause the origin of infant/child/adolescent survival adaptations to the family environment, You are the only one who can change your codependent characteristics now. You are now responsible for healing, nurture, and take care of your inner wounded child ~ and your Self.

The pain of being abused lied to, cheated on, neglected, ignored, cursed at, rejected, made to feel invisible, or invalidated has never healed.

Codependency traits represent one's difficulties in loving, accepting, trusting, and being true to Self.

UNCOVER THE BENEFITS

Codependents carry shame, guilt, and feelings of inadequacy which lead to constantly try to please others, prove worth of Self, and seek external validation at great costs, but little reward.

Codependents are focused outward – on trying to please, help, fix, wrapped up in, and attempt to intervene or control other people and situations.

Codependents base happiness and feelings on what other people are doing rather than internal feelings and values.

Codependents don't know how to be their True Self because they never learned how. They never truly learned what they want and how to be happy with Self.

During infancy and through childhood and adolescence is when personality is forming. The core of personality is formed by the age of 5, and the years that follow are just add-on personality characteristics or traits.

Codependency is a group of personality traits or personality characteristics. They are cognitive, emotional, and behavioral patterns that affect an individual's ability to have a healthy, mutually satisfying relationship with oneself and with others. They are maladaptive patterns. However, no such disorder is recognized by the Diagnostic Statistical Manual-5 (DSM-5). However, DSM-5 does recognize the Dependent Personality Disorder.

Codependency is also known as "relationship addiction" because people with codependency characteristics often form or maintain unhealthy relationships. These unhealthy relationships are often one-sided, emotionally destructive, and/or sometimes (e.g., physically, psychologically) abusive.

Codependency developed during those important formative years as a way to cope with the trauma of any kind.

Many Codependents grew up in a family with mental illness, a family of addiction, family system dysfunction, or other problems.

Other individuals with Codependency traits appear on the surface level to have had seemingly normal childhoods, but codependent traits and behavioral patterns were passed down unknowingly by primary caregivers who were Codependents.

Other individuals with Codependency Traits have buried so deeply the wounding or painful memories of childhood that it is like amnesia and therefore stored in the subconscious.

Co-dependency often affects a spouse, a parent, sibling, friend, or co-worker of a person afflicted with alcohol or drug dependence. Originally, co-dependent was a term used to describe partners in chemical dependency, persons living with, or in a relationship with an addicted person. Similar patterns have been seen in people in relationships with chronically or mentally ill individuals. Today, however, the term has broadened to describe any co-dependent person from any dysfunctional family.

Because co-dependency is usually rooted in a person's childhood, treatment often involves exploration into early childhood issues and their relationship to current destructive behavior patterns. Treatment includes education, experiential groups, and individual and group therapy through which co-dependents rediscover themselves and identify self-defeating behavior patterns. Treatment also focuses on helping patients getting in touch with feelings that have been buried during childhood and on reconstructing family dynamics. The goal is to allow them to experience their full range of feelings again.